Tears of Promise

Tears of Promise

Naiyah Jean

MAMA'S
KITCHEN
PRESS

Tears of Promise
© 2024 Naiyah Jean
ISBN: 979-8-9893829-5-8

Published by Mama's Kitchen Press
Austin, TX / Los Angeles, CA
mamaskitchenpress.com

First Trade Paperback Original Edition, 2024

Manufactured in the United States of America

Cover design & layout design by Emily Anne Evans

To Cocoa, Kale, Kima and Lagurtha (along with the rest of my siblings).

Thank you for being there regardless of the situation.

Contents

Foreword

Dear Reader,

It is with overflowing pride that I write these words, as I reflect over the years of witnessing Naiyah's evolution from womb to womanhood. Even before she could speak, her spirit spoke volumes. Born weighing less than five pounds as a result of monoembryonic birth (twins sharing the same placenta and amniotic sac) she fought an uphill battle of various respiratory issues. So, as you can imagine when she was able to articulate, she let her voice be heard even when we pleaded she didn't.

Naiyah Jean is one of the smartest people I've ever had the pleasure of knowing, and she is also one of the most courageous. Not in a "run into a burning building" sense, but in "knowing her limitations and seeking help" sense. She can at times be quiet and reserved. It's those times I truly believe she is working out situations looking for possible answers. Once a solution presents itself, she pursues it with the zest and vigor of a lioness on the hunt. Be it her education, knitting, or novellas, Naiyah continues to give whatever opportunity presented to her the respect and dedication it deserves.

When she asked me to write this foreword, I honestly was a bit surprised. The pieces that I was able to get through casted the shadow caused by the darkness of my poor parenting. To which I must admit hurt, for no parent wants to ever be faced with those hard facts. However, I was quickly reminded that these poems rooted in truth are a reflection of being allowed to be true to herself and seeing these situations as a chance to grow for one cannot have a testimony without having a test.

This book will give you a glimpse into the mindscape of Naiyahs reality. So, make sure to pay close attention, for what you hold in your hand in her own words "is an accumulation of inner reflection and outer observation."

Nayah and her poems have changed my life for the better, not only as a father but a person seeking to be the truest version of themselves.

I know they will do the same for you.

Respectfully,

DION JAHMAL

Tears of Promise

secrets

we whispered under the lights of man-made stars
that hung from the roof,

we laughed into the late night,
turning into the early morning.

we were devils, mumbling the sins of our family,
the anger toward our brothers,
the mistakes from our father,
and the unfairness of our mother.

but at the same time we spoke with the innocent angels,
memories dripped from our tongues as laughter filled our lungs.

other times more,
we were just mere mortals, wondering if God ever existed as tears of trauma escaped our hearts.

we sat on the brown blanket on my tall bed,
a cage to secrets never spoken again.

Sweet 17

17 years but I still feel seven.

I wonder what those 10 years were for.

I know 4 of them shrunk me,
Making it feel like I was smaller than 3.

I wish I could go back,
To know where all those years went.

Because I don't feel tall enough for 17,
I don't feel naive enough for 3.

I'm not a teenager, I'm a child
But I'm not a child,
I've grown out of it.

I just haven't grown into 17.

What is my why?

I must have a reason for living,
and yet I cannot find it.

I've looked through my hobbies and under my
interests,
my scattered dreams and bland beliefs,
and yet I could not find me.

I wonder,
where is it in my mind?

Maybe if I shot myself and died,
making all my memories collide,
I would find who I am inside.
But I'm not going to die to figure out if this is all a lie,
maybe I'll just cry.

Hopefully the tears will spread like ink on paper,
telling me exactly who I am,
what is my why.

Why I am alive.

Puzzle pieces

Who am I?

What about me is mine?

A stranger's face on a familiar soul,

Sewn on by a mother's womb.

A smile that I've trained to who I wanted to be by age five.

But never really mine.

Who am I?

If you broke me, I would shatter,

And the pieces that would scatter,
Would be collected back to those who matter,

Who I snapped off a piece of to fill my incompletion

All that would be left would be the pieces of me
that no one cares about, not even me, the creator.

So I beg myself to live with myself,
to find myself inside myself;
but I refuse to start digging.

I disregard myself in fear,
What if who I might find is someone I despise?

I am scared of what I might find.

Slideshow

I've lived for more than a thousand days,
and yet I can barely remember six.

flashes of rooms and smiles enter and exit my
mind like a broken slideshow,

secret of myself that I've hid from myself.

Whispers of my subconscious to my dreams,
like a telephone game to me,
the original meaning has long gone from my mind
completely.

I wonder what they were,

the memories I can't even remember,
can't even mourn the life of since I can only
remember the grave.
The only proof I have are the bits and pieces that
escaped Pandora's box.

How bad were they for my mind to try and forget
my own laughter?

Were the memories worse than my tears?

Why did God create me in such a way,
where every morning it hurts to be alive?

It's not fair to me,
I've prayed to him every night.
Why don't I get the same peace of mind as the
thieves and rapists?

Was the sin of my birth so horrible that I was
refused my birthright of peace?

Or was I just given my heirloom to mental anguish?

Why was every sorrow of the people who will not
be grieved cursed down onto me?

Shall my tears of unknown empathy fall onto black clothes,
because I have no other purpose in life except to mourn?
The souls of the dead and the damned stream into my head,
I don't know what they are saying,
I just know that it hurts to hear.

So,
I'll put a bullet to my brain,
And in the newfound emptiness,
I'll find sllence.

And in this newfound silence,
I'll find out why.

Why did God create me in such a way,
In a way I couldn't stand being alive.

Bloodletting

the metal stings, its ice-cold blade cutting through
the heat of my mind.

liter by liter blood drips out,
lightening the load of red from the rainbow

My breath becomes slower, I pray it's my last,

but I don't want to die,

I just want to kill myself.

I prayed every night to God,
to whose presence was as still as when I hold my
breath,

To end me.

But I am just a mite in a garden of stars,

Forgettable,
Unknowable,

A pest who has no purpose in the ecosystem of the universe.

But if the god I was forced to believe in humbled themselves enough to spit in my wounds, and in-between the lapse of tongue ask a question they already knew the answer to;

"Why do you do this to yourself, I created you?"

I will answer,

"It is because you created me, it is because I am alive."

Because my emotions of an infinite mind are trapped into a space of finite areas that I am unable to explain, but in need to get rid of before I explode.

So I grab a creation you made beside me, the one you loved enough to give it purpose,

A knife.

And I slice it horizontally across my wrist,
I don't want results, I just want blood.

Tears stained red from my beating heart, they
streak down my arm from the tear ducts that
sprung forth from self-inflicted violence,

And I sob not from sadness but from relief as
pressure from my mind leaks out of my wounds.

'Just cut a little deeper, then maybe the pressure
will be gone forever'

But I don't want to die,

No no no.

I just want to kill myself,
Because then I will feel alive.

I'll rip myself apart, in search of me,

To perform an emotional autopsy

shifting my intestines to find where I put my
hunger for life,

I'll drag my fingernails a top my brain,
Scratching it in wonder,

Where had I put myself?

Gouging out my eyes to see for myself what they
saw in me,
Somehow, a life worth living.

Soul searching is not enough,
I need to see why my heart beats.

I don't want to end my life,
just end myself,
to find myself,

To kill myself to live.

Tears look better on a pretty face

Thank God I look so pretty cryin',
the way your words cause these tears to fall.

Makes this saltwater burn down my cheeks,
at least the red looks good underneath these eyes
of mine.

I just wish my hands weren't too busy shakin',
so I could wipe these tears to see your face.

It's pathetic how I still love you,
regardless of the times I felt my heart in your
hands.

You've crushed it so many times,
I think I'm dyin'
I wonder if I'll look as pretty dead.
I'll fall asleep and see,
just promise that you'll be more careful with my
body,
than your words have ever been with me.

◊

A [my] mother's love fuels my guilt

Why do I want to hug death so tightly
when she holds me so dearly?

How dare the same thoughts enter the head she
kisses goodnight.

To cut the skin she created is to cut her,
So why do I yearn for a knife?

But I still stood at that cliff,
But those thoughts still screamed at me,
But I still have those scars.

And I'm so sorry you love me more than I do,
And I'm so sorry I can't love me the same.

But stop,
please stop,
I hate how much you love me,
how much you care,
then I can't hate myself without knowing how
much you don't.

It's not fair, I hate to see you cry
I don't like that I caused them.

I'm sorry mommy, please forgive me
I didn't mean it even though I did.

Dead weight

I wonder if the earth ripped out your wings,
or was it God that caused you to fall so hard?

But I know it's me who keeps you here,
stuck in a place that keeps your feathers from
growing,
keeps them molting.

I'm sorry you had me,
landed to birth me,
looked up at the sky wanting to fly but you stayed
to raise me.

If I hadn't been born, I bet you'd fly so high,
You'd be watching the world as you danced
across the sky.
I wish you'd leave,
to use those wings and fly

So I could see you soar above me far into the sky.

But unfortunately, I was one of the dreams you
had,
the only one you accomplished.

I'll give you my small wings,
so please fly.

Buried alive

What happens to you when you become like this?
Barely moving except the rise and fall of your
chest.

When you do move, you move like a zombie,
living only because you're alive.

You're tired, aren't you?

your lungs are tired of breathing,
your heart is tired of beating,

you're exhausted.

A living corpse.

It's killing you, isn't it?

Being like this, living only because you're alive,
not really wanting to die, but feeling like that is the
only option.

Are you dead yet?

It certainly smells like you are,
reeking of rotting flesh,
emotions eat at you.

Should I hold a funeral?
It feels like I will never get you back.

Your bed shall be your grave,
six feet under blankets.
The headboard your tombstone:

"Here lies she, whose body is here, but soul is gone."

History repeater

History repeats itself,
because you are now a mother.

And I am now your daughter.

So why don't—
So why can't you give me the same grace you
wish they had given you?

Aren't I your second chance?

I'm like you in more ways than one,
more ways than I wish to be.

More ways bad than good.

I am you almost through and through.

So treat me like you wish she had treated you.

History is repeating itself,
I'm starting to hate you as much as you hate your
mother.

I wish I wasn't you,
The way you prayed you didn't want to be her.

But History is repeating itself,
As it always does.

Hopefully I'll drink myself to death,
Like you two have already done.

shellshock

you say you are not afraid of them anymore,

but you ignore the bangs from a different door.

but i still count the bullets in their hands, and
tremble as i watch as each takes their stance.

that string of fate pulls taut, i fear it might break,

but i say nothing though, cause i don't want to
have a gun down my throat.

five feet apart, just like on their wedding day.

mom draws first,

but dad shoots faster,

BANG!

shoots her dead,
in her bed

she whines weak cries as blood trickles from her
eyes,

he stays silent,

wipes the blood on pages and calls it poetry,

spoken word, though never says anything about
her.

and i stand there,

shellshocked.

shellshocked, as i try to ignore the echo of ringing
by replacing them with headphones filled with the
sounds of ignorance.

shellshocked, as my sister walks into the trenches
of the living room, and wipes the spilt blood,
her soul now stained with the color of her broken
mother.

I picked up a shell, in shock, the shape of the metal
burned into my mind.

My mind, which wonders if this is right, to stay in this
this war-torn home, whose peace is stretched tight,

tight around my head, suffocating me with lies,
lies of alliances,

forgiveness filled with falsity,
poisonous apologies that I once gulped down, in
hopes of an antidote,
but now sip gingerly, still in hope.

hope that this battle is the last one,

but as i squeeze the bullet in my hand,
the ring of screams scratching at my mind.

About the Author

"Whoops, i tripped and fell right into my dreams."

Naiyah is from Big Bear, California
and lives with her 7 figure family
and 4 dogs. She likes many things,
but her love above loves would be
writing, especially when it's fun.

mamaskitchenpress.com

Mama's Kitchen Press believes that stories affirm our humanity. It is our mission to publish stories that are personal, heartfelt, and intimate.

youthwriterscamp.com

This book was created as part of Youth Writer's Camp, a program that follows a 10-Week Social-Emotional Curriculum promoting positive mental health, educational, and economic outcomes among youth.

The aim of Youth Writer's Camp is to:
• Teach adaptive social and emotion regulation skills
• Improve effective communication skills
• Increase literacy skills through creative written expression
• Empower youth by amplifying their voices to tell their stories
• Support each youth in becoming a published writer